PRAYERS THAT DESTROY DEPRESSION

PRAYERS THAT BREAK DEPRESSION AND BRING SUPERNATURAL PEACE

I.R. Womack

I.R. Womack
P.O. Box 894
Edgewood, MD 21040

TABLE OF CONTENTS

INTRODUCTION

If you are fighting against depression, you are not alone. Some of the greatest people mentioned in the Bible, including David, Elijah, Job, Moses, and Peter had to deal with depression at some point in their lives. In today's society, it is reported that 1 in 10 Americans are affected by depression at one point or another.

Depression is often the emotional or physical result of feeling anxiety, desperation, or hopelessness over a prolonged period of time. The good news is that we can defeat depression by going to the Word of God and praying in accordance with the Scriptures. The Word of God is the sword of the Spirit (Ephesians 6:17). If you use the sword of the

Spirit skillfully, you can wage war and win the battle against depression.

THE WORD TRANSFORMS YOUR WAY OF THINKING

"...but let God transform you into a new person by changing the way you think."
(Romans 12:2 NIV)

The word *transform* in the Scripture above comes from a Greek word that describes a caterpillar's metamorphosis into a butterfly. When the butterfly takes flight, it sees the world from a different vantage point than it did as a caterpillar. In much the same way, when our minds are transformed by the Word of God, we will view the circumstances in our lives from another perspective. This new perspective will cause us to be confident, hopeful, and full of God's peace and joy, even in the midst of adverse situations.

DEPRESSION IS A SPIRIT

"To appoint unto them that mourn in Zion, to give unto them beauty for ashes, the oil of joy for mourning, the garment of praise for the spirit of heaviness..." (Isaiah 61:3)

The root of depression is not always in the mind or emotions. Depression is also a spirit. This evil spirit studies people to understand their strengths and weaknesses. It looks for an open door into a person's life to enter in, build a stronghold, and afflict him/her with depression. Therefore, one must implement spiritual warfare tactics to neutralize this spirit's influence over his/her life and cast it out.

DEMON GROUPINGS

Demons rarely operate alone. They will usually work in groups to fortify their position in an individual's life. There are other spirits that are closely associated with the spirit of depression. They can be identified by how they manifest in people's lives. In order to be totally delivered, you will often have to bind and cast out the whole cluster. Here's a short list of evil spirits that are associated with depression: **anxiety**, **death**, **despair**, **despondency**, **defeatism**, **dejection**, **discouragement**, **heaviness**, **hopelessness**, **insomnia**, **morbidity**, **suicide,** and **worry**.

Victory over depression will come when we tear down all the strongholds in our minds erected by evil spirits, bind and cast them out in the authority of Jesus Christ, and renew our minds in the Word of God. As you pray these prayers with faith and fervor, and meditate upon God's Word, may the Lord grant you His peace, joy, and total victory over depression.

HOW TO USE THIS BOOK

In order to get the best results from this book, it is important that you not only recite the prayers in this book, but also internalize them and make them specific to your issues. Be certain to refer to the corresponding Scriptures and meditate on them. We are commanded by God to meditate upon His Word. The Word of God equips us to make our way prosperous and be successful in our endeavors. (Joshua 1:8)

As you pray these prayers, know that things are immediately shifting in your favor. It is vital that you understand that you are not praying in order to get God to do something that He has not already done. On the contrary, these prayers will help you to *appropriate* the healing, deliverance, and victory that Jesus Christ has **already** won for you on the Cross. *"Surely he took up our pain and bore our suffering...the punishment that brought us peace was on him, and by his wounds we are healed."* (Isaiah 53: 4-5 NIV)

This book is not only filled with powerful prayers; it also contains *mountain moving* decrees and declarations. You have authority from God to issue decrees and declarations according to His Word. When you do this in faith and understanding of your God-given authority, unseen forces will begin to move on your behalf. When you issue decrees and declarations directed toward yourself, your thoughts, emotions, and will begin to come into alignment according to what you have spoken. The Scriptures assure us that, *"You will also declare a thing, and it will be established for you; so light will shine in your ways."* (Job 22:28 KJV)

Combining fasting with fervent prayer is often necessary to deal with very challenging circumstances or stubborn demons. Be guided by the Holy Spirit as to what the requisite fast consists of to deal successfully with your condition. *"But this kind does not go out except by prayer and fasting."* (Matthew 17:21 KJV)

While praying the *spiritual warfare* prayers in this book, understand that every born-again believer has authority over demons. You don't have to stand around idly while the agents of hell are afflicting you with depression. You can destroy the works of the devil. You can bind demons and cast them out of your life in the authority of Jesus' Name.

PRAYERS, DECREES, AND FAITH DECLARATIONS

I decree and declare that I will not meditate on any negative thoughts. According to Philippians 4:8, I will only meditate on thoughts that are noble, pure, lovely, and admirable, in the mighty name of Jesus Christ.

The Lord Himself goes before me and is with me at all times. Therefore, I decree and declare that I will not be depressed.
(Deuteronomy 31:8)

I thank you, Heavenly Father, for the promise you made in your Word that you will never leave or forsake me. In your Divine Presence I am at peace.
(Deuteronomy 31:8)

Lord, I thank you for hearing my cry unto you and that you are delivering me out of all of my troubles. (Psalm 34:17)

I decree and declare that I shall not be depressed because of the challenges that I am facing. I will wait patiently for the Lord to break through on my behalf. (Psalm 40:1)

I will not be depressed, for the Lord has put a new song in my mouth; a hymn of praise unto my God! (Psalm 40:3)

The Lord shields me from every spirit of depression and lifts my head high. (Psalm 3:3)

I decree and declare that I shall not be depressed, because I have cast all my cares and anxieties upon the Lord. He has, in turn, cast His joy and peace upon me. (1 Peter 5:6-7)

In the midst of my issues and the troubles of life, I have the peace of God. (John 16:33)

I decree and declare that I shall not be depressed, because God shows me compassion and gives me comfort in all of my troubles.
(2 Corinthians 1:3-4)

In the Name of Jesus Christ, I decree and declare that I will not be depressed over the issues and troubles of life. Instead, I will rejoice, because I'm participating in the sufferings of Christ and will be overjoyed when His Glory is revealed.
(1 Peter 4:12-113)

I shall not be depressed, because I know that the Lord is strengthening me, helping me, and upholding me with His right hand.
(Isaiah 41:10)

The Lord turns all darkness in my life into light. Therefore, I will not be discouraged, weighed down, or depressed, in Jesus' Name.
(2 Samuel 22:29)

The Lord has strengthened my heart (mind, will, and emotions) to wait patiently until change comes to my situation. (Psalm 27:14)

Heavenly Father, according to Psalm 147:3, I ask you to heal my broken heart and bind up my wounds. I receive my healing in Jesus' Name with thanksgiving.

Heavenly Father, I thank you for comforting me during my trials and tribulations. Despite what I am going through, I will not become self-absorbed. I will comfort others going through hardships with the same comfort that I receive from you, in Jesus' Name. (2 Corinthians 1:4)

Although I've sown tears, I shall reap with songs of joy! (Psalm 126:5)

According to 2 Corinthians 10:4, I tear down every stronghold of depression erected in my mind by evil spirits, in the Name of Jesus Christ.

In name of Jesus Christ, I take captive every thought that has caused me to be depressed. (2 Corinthians 10:5)

According to Nehemiah 8:10, I decree and declare that the joy of the Lord is my strength. Therefore, no spirit of depression can overtake me, in Jesus' Name.

Oh Lord, let there be a wall of fire around my mind to protect my thoughts and life from all psychic suggestions from the enemy that cause depression, in Jesus' Name.

I appropriate the blood of Jesus Christ to my mind. No spirit of depression can enter in because of His blood.

Lord, because you delivered me, I am no longer crushed in spirit. (Psalm 34:18)

I decree and declare that my hope is in God. My soul shall not be downcast, in Jesus' Name. (Psalm 43:5)

In the Name of Jesus Christ, I decree and declare that I shall no longer be depressed, because my soul has found rest in Him.
(Psalm 62:5)

SPIRITUAL WARFARE PRAYERS

I bind every spirit of heaviness and depression and cast you out of my life, in the mighty name of Jesus Christ.

I take authority over every spirit of anxiety that is working with depression against me. I bind you and cast you out of my life in Jesus' Name.

I take authority over every spirit of death that is working with depression against me. I bind you and cast you out of my life in Jesus' Name. According to Psalm 118:17, I decree and declare that I shall not die, but live and declare the works of the Lord!

I take authority over every spirit of despair that is working with depression against me. I bind you and cast you out of my life in Jesus' Name. According to 2 Corinthians 4:8, I decree and declare that although I may be facing troubles from every side, I will not be in despair, in Jesus' Name.

I take authority over every spirit of despondency working with depression against me. I bind you and cast you out of my life in Jesus' Name. According to Joshua 1:9, I decree and declare that I am strong and of good courage, for the Lord is with me wherever I go.

I take authority over every spirit of defeatism working with depression against me. I bind you and cast you out of my life in Jesus' Name. According to 1 John 5:4, I decree and declare that, by my faith in Jesus Christ, I have already overcome the world!

I take authority over every spirit of dejection working with depression against me. I bind you and cast you out of my life in Jesus' Name. According to Philippians 4:7, I decree and declare that the peace of God that transcends all understanding is guarding my heart and mind, in the name of Christ Jesus.

I take authority over every spirit of discouragement working with depression against me. I bind you and cast you out of my life in Jesus' Name. According to Romans 8:28, I lift my head high and rejoice in the midst of my trials, knowing that God is causing them to work together for my good.

I take authority over every spirit of heaviness working with depression against me. I bind you and cast you out of my life in the mighty name of Jesus Christ. Lord Jesus, I thank you for delivering me from the spirit of heaviness and have given me a garment of praise. I glorify your Holy Name! Hallelujah!

I take authority over every spirit of hope-lessness working with depression against me. I bind you and cast you out of my life in the mighty name of Jesus Christ. Lord, ac-cording to Psalm 16:9, I will rest in hope, and my hope is in you.

I decree and declare that my hope shall never be cut off.

Heavenly Father, according to Psalm 119:147, I have put my hope in your Word. I receive every blessing and promise that you have assured me in your Word. I will not be hopeless or depressed in the midst of my cir-cumstances, because your Word cannot fail. It will accomplish all that you desire, and prosper wherever you send it. (Isaiah 55:11)

I take authority over every spirit of insomnia working with depression against me. I bind you and cast you out of my life in the mighty name of Jesus Christ. I decree and declare that I shall never again be robbed of my

sleep, because the Lord grants sleep to those He loves.
(Psalm 127:2)

According to Proverbs 3:24, I decree and declare that when I lie down to rest at night, my sleep will be sweet.

I take authority over every spirit of morbidity working with depression against me. I tear down and destroy every stronghold you have erected in my mind. I bind and cast you out of my life in Jesus' Name.

According to 1 Corinthians 2:16, I decree and declare that I have the mind of Christ. Therefore, no ungodly thoughts from the enemy will take root in my mind.

I thank you, Lord, that you have promised me peace. I receive your peace with thanksgiving, and decree and declare that I shall not be tormented with any morbid thoughts, in Jesus' Name.

I take authority over every spirit of suicide working with depression within me. I bind you, cast you out, and close every spiritual doorway that you exploited to enter into my life, in Jesus' Name.

Lord Jesus, I thank you for coming to earth to give me an abundant life. I receive a life of prosperity and peace with thanksgiving, in your Holy Name. (John 10:10)

I decree and declare that I shall not abort God's purpose for my life by committing suicide. I will fight the good fight of faith and take hold of eternal life, in Jesus' Name.
(1 Timothy 6:12)

I will fight the good fight, finish my course, and keep the faith, in Jesus' Name!
(2 Timothy 4:7)

I take authority over every spirit of worry afflicting me. I bind you and cast you out of my life, in the name of Jesus Christ.

I will not worry about anything. Instead, I will pray about everything with thanksgiving. By doing so, I will experience the peace of God that surpasses all understanding, in Jesus' mighty Name! (Philippians 4:6-7)

I close every spiritual doorway that evil spirits have exploited to afflict me with depression, in Jesus' mighty Name.

PRACTICAL TIPS

I'd be remiss if I did not give you some helpful tips to accompany prayer in battling depression. Attacking depression from multiple angles will help to secure a long lasting victory.

DIET & EXERCISE

"Do you not know that your bodies are temples of the Holy Spirit, who is in you, whom you have received from God?"
(1 Corinthians 6:19 NIV)

Your body is the temple of the Holy Spirit. Taking care of your body by exercising regularly yields great results, not only for your physical body, but also for your soul (mind, will, and emotions). Exercise is a powerful weapon against depression. Research suggests that exercise can be just as effective as antidepressants at decreasing fatigue and boosting energy levels. Physical activity increases mood-enhancing endorphins and reduces stress. Even a light 10-15 minute workout can make a great difference in alleviating the symptoms of depression. Get moving!

As equally important as getting exercise is your diet. The foods you eat have a direct impact on the way you feel. Eat foods that are high in omega-3 fats, magnesium, complex carbs, tryptophan, and vitamin B. They can help decrease anxiety and boost your serotonin (feel good) levels, give you energy, and provide an overall sense of well-being. Decrease your intake of foods that are high in sugar and refined carbs. They make you feel good for a moment, but then make your mood and energy levels crash quickly.

DON'T BECOME A HERMIT

"Praise be to the God and Father of our Lord Jesus Christ, the Father of compassion and the God of all comfort, who comforts us in all our troubles, so that we can comfort those in any trouble with the comfort we ourselves receive from God."
(2 Corinthians 1:3-4 NIV)

When you're depressed it's very easy to become self-absorbed and isolated, and begin meditating on everything that is negative or out place in your life. The Scripture above is very clear on how to remedy this. Receive the comfort that God gives to those who are in fellowship with Him through prayer and worship. Then, take that same comfort and be a blessing to someone else who is in need of comfort or a helping hand. It's very hard to remain depressed when you're busy being a blessing to someone else. You'll quickly find that when you help uplift others you are also uplifted. *"The generous will prosper; those who refresh others will themselves be refreshed."* (Proverbs 11:25 NLT) There are plenty of places where you can go and plenty of organizations to join that will give you the privilege of ministering to others. Your local church, food pantry or homeless shelter, are great places to start.

GET PROFESSIONAL HELP

"Get all the advice and instruction you can, so you will be wise the rest of your life."
(Proverbs 19:20 NLT)

If you are feeling overwhelmed or find that your condition is getting worse, then by all means get help. You don't have to face this issue alone. Seek professional help from someone who has good credentials and a proven track record in dealing with your condition. Go to your spiritual leaders and mentors for counsel and prayer as well, even if they are not certified in dealing with de-pression on a clinical level. As we have al-ready established in this book, anointed prayers will prove to be highly effective. To have a team of intercessors who are covering you in prayer will compound their results.

CONCLUSION

Thank you for ordering a copy of this book. May you experience total peace and freedom, in Jesus' Name. I have personally applied the prayers and principals in this book and they have proved to be invaluable.

If you have enjoyed this book and want to spread the good word, please rate and review it on Amazon. Thanks again!

In Christ's Service,

I.R. Womack

OTHER BOOKS BY I.R. WOMACK ON AMAZON

DELIVERANCE MINISTRY BASIC TRAING: Learn How To Cast Out Demons & Set the Captives Free

FIVEFOLD MINISTRY BASIC TRAINING: Understanding the distinct roles and functions of apostles, prophets, evangelists, pastors and teachers

ABOUT THE AUTHOR

I.R. Womack is a teacher, preacher, and missionary. He is founder of the Kingdom Ministry Institute. He travels internationally, conducting miracle crusades and training the body of Christ and organizations in various areas, including: Fivefold ministry, healing ministry, deliverance ministry, prophetic ministry, entrepreneurship, and financial empowerment. He is married to Shavonne Womack and they have four children.

INVITE I.R. WOMACK

If you would like to invite I.R. Womack to speak at one of your events, click this link and leave a detailed message on the online contact form.

www.irwomackministries.org

Made in the USA
Middletown, DE
28 April 2018